Alvin Greenberg

DARK
LANDS

DARK LANDS

a book of poems by

Alvin Greenberg

Other books by Alvin Greenberg:

The Small Waves
 (novel, 1965, El Corno Emplumado)

The Metaphysical Giraffe
 (poems, 1968, New Rivers Press)

Going Nowhere
 (novel, 1971, Simon & Schuster)

The House of the Would-be Gardener
 (poems, 1972, New Rivers Press)

Acknowledgement is gratefully made to the editors of the following magazines for permission to reprint poems which originally appeared in their pages: *Akademi, Antioch Review, December, El Corno Emplumado, Epoch, Fragments, Hearse, The Little Magazine, The Minnesota Review, New: American & Canadian Poetry, Poetry, Poetry Northwest, Quartet, Red Cedar Review, Seneca Review, South Florida Poetry Journal, Sou'wester, Spirit, Trace,* and *West Coast Review.*

ITHACA HOUSE
108 N. PLAIN STREET
ITHACA, N.Y., 14850

Dark Lands

CONTENTS

for marsha

and

all the places

From this the poem springs: that we live in a place
That is not our own . . .

Wallace Stevens
"Notes Toward a Supreme Fiction"

i

The partaker partakes of that which changes him.
The child that touches takes character from the thing,
The body, it touches.

Wallace Stevens
"Notes Toward a Supreme Fiction"

foreign markets

i don't recognize the brand
i can't understand the price
but i'll try the stuff anyway:

it may do me some good,
and good's what i need.

arhythmia

the initial drum drums
names, to begin with,
and hollow reply cries,

here i am!   but where
is that? another answers,
is it enough? and what's

the rhythm?   no one
begins a silent dance,
making with body what

words can't move, no
one accepts the harsh
demand, that words

alone are uncertain
good, that only the body
of noise is left, noise

the format of a still
less certain brotherhood:
the shrill of children

singing from the roofs,
temple bells roaring
through the long mid-

night, then the sullen
flap of crows at dawn
shedding the darkness

in heavy flight, loud
daytime coming on, full
of lucid names, screech

of flesh on flesh or
rasp of bone on bone.

structural flaws

bars on the windows,
she said, scorpions
behind the bathroom
door,
      don't think i
like this sad foreign
architecture   any
more.

never mind the bars,
he said, some windows
have to be like that;
there's no getting
out, nor any getting
in,
   just that striped
reminder on the floor
with each afternoon
sun:
      things that aren't
the way they'd be if
we rebuilt this place
again.

as for the scorpions,
well, they both agreed
that something had to
go:
     granted the damned
things fled on sight,
even the thought they
left on the run said,
no.

dark land/
black poems

i.

heard my own old
name come bucking up
from palm-tree forests:
saipah! (o boss!

white man! master!)
and that was just the
children, black as fear

they roused in me,
passing the giggle
of my arrival on
down the road: shit,

kids, knock it off!
names are tough to
live with and i
didn't ask for mine.

ii.

the black jews of cochin
see this dirt, stand
kneedeep in the red clay,

send long green creepers
out to visit the synagogue,
buy bones and whiskey

at the white white shops,
roots churning as they sniff
old dry temptations
off the yellow desert.

themselves they hack
for cuttings, turning
blacker with each stroke,
sing out in pain beneath

the rusty knife, and scatter
about their coarse dark roots
the dark manure of old
words, rhythms, prayers,
lusts, greeds: all black.

iii.

now it's these black
crows, crows black
as my bad blood
(that fakes in cuts

a life as red as yours
though i know better),
that take this place.

from first light on
they batter dumbly
upward on thick wings,

never soar, but get
there all the same:
they have the morning

then, their clumsy
chunk of sky, first
pick of garbage and
the last black caw.

new delhi zoo

it's a long way between
animals and for the animals
it's a long way between

people, and that leaves
them more serene: so when
you come upon the rhino

motionless among green
shrubs you see nothing.
closer, the moat appears,

suggesting some reality
of shape. 'dangerous
when disturbed'? who's

disturbed when nothing's
here except one monster
given over to solemnity

and far off the silent
decadent white tiger and
in between, nothing in

between, nothing except
vast distances, vast
distances between one

still beast and another.

old carvings we attempt to come by honestly

what we've composed
one life around's
a house, one house

around its walls,
life figured on
those walls in wood
and distances, bare

assed old wooden
maidens mount our
walls and spread
their legs, clefts

dripping a powdery
dry rain of termite
leavings, a dead

mound on the floor,
dry old mess to be
swept up, a fall of
ancient girls, o

can't you make it
any longer up there
on our walls? o

you ladies heaping
your dry leavings
ever floorward, o

ladies opening from
wall to ground, o

you rotten, hollow
bitches whom even
termites can get

around, come pose
your old bowlegged
stance up there on
our walls, lift

those gouged out
holes above us on
the walls, rain

down on us, off
our walls, those
powdery leavings
as you decompose.

the black jew

(cochin, india)

i.

he swept out shops
for the white master

solomon's own son
with the peeled cock

who was a trader
first and only became

a planter of jews
thereafter

ii.

he opened his mouth
to a babble of fire

bright as chilies
fell to the ark

tongue scorched dumb
woke at twilight

to da gama's ships
with filthy sails

iii.

he fought the crows
for bones, drank

the running sores
of the red clay

tugged at the knot
of dysentery

never daring to ask,
where's the toilet?

iv.

he took the bribe
at last, a free trip

and holier black dirt
to lie in but had

a real perpetual
jaundice in his eye

the yellow dietary
ache of vision

v.

and wore his liver
always on his sleeve

unless what dripped
there was his heart

those inside things
are so messy

you can hardly
tell them apart

the past and the future will be
dealt with in another lesson

a solemn translation
of beaches: one day
they're fine as talcum
and the next blackening

your soles with oil
some tanker's dumped
far out of sight, thus:
a needed demonstration

of the present tense,
the nest of sand warms
a broad-winged manta's
tedious death. 'sir,'

his captors translate,
benign with the trophy
of his tail as he gasps
and gasps, 'so valuable

fish: for the medical
college his liver, for
the market his flesh.'
and what more perfect

voice do we have for
the current offshore,
or what more accurate
transliteration of now?

climate of change

i.

the real
       weather
is there, a first

discovery of travel,
climate of change
after such long
flight, one truly

lucid day,
       indian
glare or mexican
fragility of vision
in the thin
       air:
clarity of not just
mountains but sea-
floor as well, the
lurching hermit in
his stolen spiral
shell; then
       night
and all those god-
damned stars, and
those fiery holes
burned in our bodies
by one night's lying
on the roof beneath
them; then small

clouds coming on
inland, their high
dark winds
       forecast
of another time.

ii.

last of all there
comes the return:
smog in new york,
fog in seattle,
snow in st. paul.
these are foreign
places, these are

our foreign homes,
and there the air

is think, it has

due weight, we go
into its bearing

down, we're borne
so quickly down
by jet into that
murk out of the
high hard far off
glare there's only
time to snatch dark

glasses off and see
and see or try to

see the weather we
now know:
                    beneath
the skin the isobars
of pain,
          the high
that creeps along
behind the low.

to the end now

the end is deep
inside and both
of us go looking
for it there. ah
ha, end, we come,
we come! but it
slips on beyond
and together we
stand and watch
it go. o end we

shall be coming
after, now. and
if it's not at
the end that we
say goodbye, we
may say goodbye
now, to the end.
all of a sudden
a thunderstorm
passes. smack go
the trees. is it
the end? it goes

but we are still
looking. however,
there are limits,
there are limits,
and from ground

level — where we
are sitting just
now — a receding
horizon goes on
receding. storms
do too. not at
all less useful
because so, ah,

recessional. but
behind one range
of mountains off
there, is there,
perhaps, not any
thing? and if it
is so, is it not
the end? anyway,
we're off to see.
round and round:
we consider this

a mission filled
with danger, for
if they're right
that everything
smacks of the end,
of what does that
end smack? it is
more tiring than
debates to climb
those mountains.
let some far-off

sightings bring
the end near. ah,
what resolution!

oh, what loss of
depth. and will
it wait till we
arrive? apples
of kashmir we'll
find there, just
like the little
ones in our back
yard, where rises
our very slight
hill with trees
that, when they
bear, bear apples
but don't always

have such ends.
not always. that
is their limit,
but could such a
limit be an end?
is it resolved
that an end etc
reveals to all
its coming by
being here all
the time? such
a thought! such

round and round-
ness, eh? did we
try such foreign
delicacies smack
smack? what is
the flavor that
no man mentions?
no. what's that
flavor everyone
talks about but
no one savors?

the one we look
for undistorted
grows right here
somewhere, near
by and clear as
mountain without
lens or haze. do
you remember that
storm? hailstones
have gunned down
half the apples.
see the endless
debate, too! but
little things,
on this ground,
around our feet:
they are what's
here, now, what
ever their taste.

ii

Each must take the other as a sign, short sign
To stop the whirlwind, balk the elements.

Wallace Stevens
"Notes Toward a Supreme Fiction"

fire sermon

after the long, slow passage of our fucking
we watch the gulls,
the true owners of lake superior,
fondling the wind as they move into it.

over and over we repeat the name of the town
'tofte . . . tofte . . . tofte . . .'
till at last it grows warm and firm between us.

then the gulls come by once more,
in the opposite direction.
this time it is the wind that handles *them*.

this wind.
this day and place.
this poem

is a poem you can light a fire with:

all you have to do is tear it out
and touch a match to it.
with a torch like that
you can set worlds aflame.

for one who doesn't like games

she's my own duffer,
goes at it with a nine
iron, hacks and hacks but
cannot raise the damned
thing from the sand trap.
never mind, i say, pick it
up and toss it on the green.
her shoes are full of sand,
she shudders at the cool
wind on her sweaty body,
cannot bend and pleads
fatigue. cheat! i enthuse,
tossing the ball up to
the green. she trudges
joylessly after, no believer
in my strategy. you can't
do it like that, she mutters,
fishing in her bag. oh!
she knows this game. still,
there's something of a smile
there as she lines her putter
up. the old ball, in equal
pain, grins broadly back.
with one smooth jab she
sinks it. by god! a thirty
footer! it takes me three:
i drive like hell but
have no confidence on
the greens, so all in all
our scores come out about
the same. we play in street
shoes and carry our own
bags. old duffer, she pants
as we cross to the twelfth
tee, what a goddam lousy game.

the book of changes

(for matt, nick, and ann)

> "One might say that person-
> ality at the first stage
> crystallizes around the con-
> viction 'I am what I am given,'
> and that of the second, 'I am
> what I will.' The third can be
> characterized by 'I am what I
> can imagine I will be.' "
> —Erik Erikson

i.

this is the first child;
what he sees, he sees first.
all comes down to him:

candles, disdain, foreign countries
descend upon him. he bends
his head, but they
settle into his open arms,

melt, are gone into him.
he raises his head then.
clouds gather above him
and changes play upon his face.

his arms remain extended.

ii.

this is the second child,
all in his own own time.
his smile is an umbrella

which renders him impervious
to the descent of candles,
shame, foreign countries. his arms

dangling loosely at his sides,
he watches all go by.
not till he's ready

does he step forward at last
through the fallen clutter,
still smiling the same smile.

iii.

this is the third child
and she runs like mad
dragging behind her
a great clutter of candles,
torment, foreign countries
hung out like tin cans
on a tangled string
of her own unwinding.

when she pauses, everything
settles heaped around her.

amazed by such profusion,
she hides her head in her hands.

when she bares it again it is
solemn, and considerably older.

knowing what it is you say you are

a drag is a kind
of an anchor, it

ties you down in
high seas   says

o: there you are.

the mad bomber of havoc, minn.

hours after the explosion
i am still fiddling
with fragments of the fuse.

animals come and go,
sniffing among the ruins,
their appetites awakened by the red

glow of disaster.
little enough they find
to gnaw on: only the bloodless

man still bent over the pieces
of the beginning.
he ought to be asking questions:

was this the desired result?
was it the only way?
but he just fondles the pieces,

seeing how they fail to fit together,
not even aware of the animals
who pad softly by,

ignoring him.
i'll ignore him too.
i'll go off with the animals.

a dance from the floating island

as with gulliver
the musics that
we traveled in
were all discord

    therefore we
listened closely
and so made our
dance, in which
we all held bony

hands inside this
flesh inside of
which we danced
and danced and

were this circle
of our own flesh
dancing, dancing,
until one dancer
asked, 'what is

this ridiculous
rhythm that we
dance? thum, hup,
clop, bom — never
a repetition or

a round?' we were
astounded but we
didn't stop. we
knew the way it
went within this

flesh, and that
way we went too:
thup, clom, hom,
bot, and it *was*

a circle, after
all! for in it
we moved those
bones together
and those bones,
they moved apart.

what we carry with us, we are

these here things
are not the bones
of contention and

if they are, it's
not with warlike
intention at all,

so if they rattle,
they rattle. maybe
we rattle them. it

isn't music, o no,
but makes a sound
that's quite *like*

music all the same:
thump thump (then
still). if no one

sees them, they'll
make the strangest
noise of all. *clop*

clop, they pound,
together, and yet,
amazingly, don't

shatter and fall,
but clank, thump,
clop, never quite

with rhythm, but
rhythm isn't all.

a geophysical poem for my children

this is the father
who is all thumbs
in the workshop.

these are the moons
he has made in
spite of the thumbs.

there are the nearly
circular orbits in
which they stay aloft.

that is a genuine
surprise. and this—
a continental drift:

o just touch me
and feel how strong
the tidal pull is.

an anniversary lost in travel

by tuesday it was too
late already, we'd been
on and off half a dozen
planes, the permanent
fix of tourism lodged
in our veins, so we had

missed the day, it was
neither a take-off nor
a landing, but should

have been a pause — i'm
the one who's forever
checking the tickets:
are they in my pocket?
where to next? weren't
we supposed to gawk at

something here? what
do we carry that gets
lost in the mechanics
of travel, if not you

and i, for the children
are all in their seats,
safety belts fastened,
then sudden the plane

gives a lurch. what was
that? just a familiar

feeling in the stomach,
in our familiar science

fiction it could have
been the sickening jolt
of a man plunging from
one space-time continuum
to another, and wheeeee

away we go, into what
forgetfulness and what
world now? o baby tell
me, are you ready for
all this alien stuff?

the inland sea

no longer even a michigan or superior
i go on for miles and miles
with ships lost on my surface,
out of sight of land,
above schools of unknown fish.

then i shrink and dry.
sailors *walk* ashore from their stranded ships!
the israelites flee across among dying fish
with the arabs in hot pursuit,
laughing at the threat of water.

how i'd like to send great waves
crashing in on both of them!
but the best i can manage is a tiny trickle,
little more than a tear.

it will be months before i fill again
to the point where my own son
can float his home-made raft here.

the wishing well

listen: we lean over this darkness
from the same side, saying the words
that bring our heads closer

when out of my mouth flutter
the sparrows of distraction.

you flail at them in disbelief
till the air is full of grey feathers
and we are both tumbling:

through the feathers the words fall,
singing their own songs,
and we fall through the words

into the flesh of our own soft
landing.   listen: there
are no birds we need to live among.

listen: it's dark but here
everything cushions everything else.

egg dream

(for ann)

in the sunlight you stood
on my shoulders, lifting
your head among branches

to discover the nest. how
blue! you cried, and i was
satisfied. how lonely! and

i quickly brought you down.

but now in the night you
come with the egg in your
hands, crying *see! see!*

like the bird its mother.

prayer for a lost sense

if you could *really* smell me you'd know
the eight kinds of fear i exude:

fear that somewhere someone has said
    the one thing that can't be taken back
fear of travel
fear that when you wake me in the morning
    i'll look in the mirror and see
    that you've woken the wrong person
fear that there's some fear in you
    that i can't see or hear
fear of staying in one place forever
fear that there are tanks in the streets
    and no one in the houses,
    near me
fear of spiders
fear of more spiders

you'd also know my twelve odors
of thought, dream, and desire

but i'll tell you about those another time:
right now i smell you and know
which way we're going today

the gamblers

we roll the dice
and when they come up 'shipwreck'
we drop the sails,
let the tide carry us in upon the reef.

do we know how to accept?

in the center of the island is a volcano.
on the wet sands of the beach we write SOS.
we eat sour breadfruit and sweet bananas.
the dice are still ours
but there's nowhere to roll them.

after many years the island begins to rumble
and we rumble with it.
it's time.
we climb the slope,
cast the dice into the fiery pit.
ourselves we roll back down to the beach

and come up swimming.

morning thoughts at night

the sun comes up over
our bed:
                    hello you
                    'hello you'
(actually it's the moon)

and somewhere out there
there's someone
who doesn't think much of all this.

if we were less selfish we'd go out after him
and smile on him with both our bodies,
regardless of what time it is.

the double agent

i entered your country in an obvious disguise,
wearing many hats and an impeccable passport.
who could have suspected *me*? i was, i thought,
the only spy within a hundred miles. and yet,
from the clumsy way you held your cigarette,
i should have known.

                  i should have known
from your open invitation to mine your harbors,
dynamite your bridges.

                  i should have known
when you brought the children, one by one, your
fingers on your lips.

                  i should have known
when you removed my penultimate hat, a homburg
many sizes too small.

                  i should have known
when your letters arrived from all directions
with uncancelled stamps.

                  i should have known
when you lay in bed in my arms at last singing
'espionage o espionage! the spy and counterspy
improve each other.'

                  i should have known,
then, that the border signs had been reversed,
the guards drugged, the alarm system retuned
to play 'hey jude!'—or was it the 'polonaise'
from bach's suite no. 2 for flute and strings?

—all so that i could find you out in the end,
a spy in your own country, waiting to decode
this message in the sweatband of my last hat,
an old straw boater: 'you should have known:
all the secret documents here are your own.'

iii

Nothing had happened because nothing had changed.
Yet the General was rubbish in the end.

> Wallace Stevens
> "Notes Toward a Supreme Fiction"

message

my friend the soldier
sends me a letter.
on the envelope
it says, 'confidential:
swallow before reading.'

the dutiful mailman
stands in the doorway,
waiting and watching.

i begin to chew
like a good citizen,
an eager correspondent
biting savagely deep
into the envelope.

but the paper: it
crackles horribly, like
flames between my teeth.

poor richard

today we open the almanack
to worship st. ben, find
the moon full, known now and
again as bomber's moon
and affording us sufficient
light to read the headlines
by until some crucial black-
out moment: find the moon
is gone, leaf through the
pages in vain, hearing
the roar far off (*they* read
by dark: high up they bank
and turn, read haste makes
waste, beginning another
run, and constant dropping
wears away stones. from
what a practiced altitude
they set their sights, read,
like sealed orders, old
advice: the cat in gloves
catches no mice: arch
and go off, purring into
exactitude of sunrise.

tomorrow they return with
diligence. they have arisen
early and found both bombs
to sell and bombs to keep.
they have great wealth
of bombs, they have
that book, they have
the time of night to
make full moons go down
and leave, for us to read
by, no other light.

a bestiary of domestic animals

the dog. the pig. the horse. god
bless them all. they laid their bones
in the furrows of humanity. but ours
we never rested. after
decades of admonishment we had
the elephant attuned to all our wants,
the giraffe vocal with delight.

now success spreads its tail among
the few remaining trees. we all
applaud: o the animal
kingdom, the animal kingdom!
then we go home to grunt and sweat
over our lawns and our wives.

for the young draftee

the elephant awakens
and all around us he
trumpets the jungle
with his loneliness.

that weathered hulk
of his goes crashing
and weeping through
impossible thickets.

trees fall. monkeys
flee. and who of us
sees his lucid, grey,
nearly extinct terror?

an impromptu home puppet show
for george washington's birthday

a green dragon on a child's hand speaks first:
'all right,' he says, 'all right,
who did this thing, who
chopped down that apple tree?'

'now let's see,' says the red
fox peeking around the edge of the couch,
'what was i supposed to do today?'

'white georges landed on plymouth rock,'
says big black dead malcolm x,
'but who did plymouth rock land on?'

'where did everybody go?' says george
from a paper bag with eyeholes and white curls,
'has anybody seen red fox today?'

the audience wildly applauds, one
four-year-old girl, compounding
heresies with her dirty hands.

the actors, however, depart on the verge of tears.
they hadn't meant the game to be so short,
but they hadn't anything else to say.

american cookery

"A number of American presidents
in this century, including the
current resident of the White
House, have prided themselves on
their culinary talents. More than
one has been found, late at night
in the big kitchen on Pennsylvania
Avenue, whipping up some strange
and private delight."

the white house chef stews in his own juices.
the woman's page labels this 'a hasty pudding'
and decries the red sauce not his own
with which he continually bastes himself.

he licks what streams down over his faces.

on a t.v. show called 'international cuisine'
he brandishes all sorts of cutlery and declares,
'the world is not a delicatessen for gourmets:
            buy mixes.'

he holds up a package of his own for display.

letter to a native land

'love,' writes our friend—
who has met at last the city

of his dreams— 'has given way
to squalor.' and yet the city

survives his disappointment.
towers and suburbs intact, it

keeps on growing. trees fade,
azaleas reappear in pots, it

struggles outward to meet with
our own far distant settlement.

we smile at its slow, awkward
movements. undoubtedly it will

bring him along. after decades
of county engineers, mulches,

potato salads, here we are in
reunion. 'squalor' hovers over

us, making our eyes smart. we
sit still and do not mention

the animals. live rats scamper
across the living room decor

and the bones of rats inhabit
the cupboards of love. 'here,'

we say, 'we are most at home,
and we do not choose to move.'

epitaph

these are the very last
words of the week. all is final:
the names of the days, their ends.

monday
the victim of overwork
tuesday
that i strangled while it still slept
wednesday and thursday
that went together in a suicide pact
friday
on which we operated with such careless haste
saturday
that took the wrong step in a drunken stupor
sunday
that languished before our very eyes
sunday
that we never appreciated till it was gone
sunday
still warm in the grave

goddamn we say these clumsy deaths
in the dark on the edge of the cliff
of the new week:

they're ours, aren't they?

iiii

He imposes orders as he thinks of them,
As the fox and snake do.

      Wallace Stevens
      "Notes Toward a Supreme Fiction"

poem

mother had poems
but what did she
do with them?
forgot to
write them down.

mother had songs
but what did she
do with them?
lost
the goddamn tune.

mother had bones
but what did she
do with them?
moved them
all around,

and that was
really something.

october at moccasin lake

beneath the northern lights
we are all transformed into
buffoons, making bad jokes

out of our embarrassment.
but is it our fault? we cry.
we blame instead a flagrant

nature full of mosquitoes,
sensitive plants, gneiss—
leaving us only the choice

of fear or laughter. a green
and white silence descends
upon us. we retreat indoors.

(for john knoepfle)

a toast

to our friend john,
who has said farewell,
for all of us, to
the passenger pigeon,
the great auk,
the green turtle, and
a whole host of slow,
ungainly creatures.

this is a 1932
cabernet sauvignon,
john,
the last bottle:

we are slow, ungainly
creatures all, and
we rise and say in unison
farewell,
john,
we do not want to go.

remnant, auction, end of season sale

there it all is: the table-
land mountain and valley
full of last season's goods,
nature in the mill end
shop or at the good will
where remnants of remnants
end, at bankruptcy auction
where nothing's a bargain,
everyone stands to lose,
it's a white elephant sale,
what use can it possibly have?
just look at those colors
which turn brown before you
know it. what's good's been
plucked long since no doubt,
too much time has passed,
frost has had the heal-all
and the rest is mismatched,
tattered, lumpy, faded,
poorly refinished, worn too thin
for either warmth or comfort,
the styles preposterous, the
seller like the sales gone
quite to seed.   old ladies
in the aisles who once in
younger days lived among
stuff like this, now only
finger dry goods and mutter
at the prices: honey, you've
got to come early or not at all.

the moon poem goes all ways

love-

stones rattle in the pouches of my heart
and beg to be polished.
i turn and turn about the center they make

feeling them tumbling there inside me.
each one i know by the nature of its edges,
each has its own hard statement to make:

will make.
the dark container of their dreams is what i am not.

all this escapes me.

the birds in my bones stretch their wings.
the wolf in my bowels is ready to spring.
this isn't the song i meant to sing.
                  this

was intended to be a poem for charlie baxter,
who was in the john
when we watched man take his first steps on the moon,

but has become instead, i see,
a poem with two tits
—one at each end—

and a bright flavor for those who care to suck on it
and are willing, when they go away,
to remember it with

love.

**poem found in a dream,
dream found in a poem**

the night comes up and
catches us, hard at work on

our horizons: beasts with horns
and children riding on

their backs pass
to and fro, and up and down,

laying their shaggy paws
noiselessly upon our ground.

the moon comes up and close
behind the moon the poem.

it has rough edges
and goes round and round,

we see it rise but we are
somewhere else when it goes down.

special delivery

the bomb squad
opens this package
and finds it was

only an old pair
of bones clicking
in the morning

mail. was that,
they ask, a
message? they are

obliged to send
them ticking
on their way.

curb your dog

piss on poetry: it's full of sharp edges,
rusty spikes that can even lead to lockjaw
and thorns too   burrs like those that stick
in dogs' coats   you don't even know they're
there and when you do and shake them loose
the seed falls on someone else's property.

next spring it's your fault he has weeds.

education

gradually, i became the author
of the theory of 'do and learn.'
before, it had been someone else.
yesterday it was my turn.

i did! i did!
i became scissors, paper, paste!
everything i wasn't
i decided to burn.

what i learned was,
to be left with what i am:

the red scrawl of 'the merely personal.'

celebration

(for bill truesdale)

look! eight people and more
trying to write a poem about
one small cabin in the woods.

just look at them slinking about
between the beavers and their trees:
are there words there?
trust them: they'll find the words.

but what about the children?
what about the dogs?
cram them all in!
and don't forget the poets' wives.

there they go! is that the
'infinitely expansible cabin of the mind'?
hell no! it's only wood and stone.
nonetheless, it opens its doors

and they all rush to get in at once.
trees and islands plunge in among them.
that's an act of creation for you.

the basket

i have a basket
in which to catch

my blood
and when my blood
runs all out
it will hold

my head
and when my head
rots and you

dump it out
you can blot
the stains with

turpentine
and fill it again
with the dry gourds

of my gut

                just

remember how i
busted my ass

weaving this thing
turning what any
child could do

into some pain
ruined my eyes
and never quite got

the handle right

just

      remember it's
a container

hang on tight
and keep it

full of someone

recipe

i have just come back from the days
when they used to put something alive
into the walls of a new building
—an old man, a child, a dog—
so it could stand up straight and say,
'i am part and parcel of the world, both
the container and the thing contained.'

and it was a long journey back
but i wanted to make a poem
and i wanted to put you in it,
marsha,
in order to keep it alive and warm
and to make sure everyone knew
how real it was.

biopsy

peel back the christmas wrapping
of three kinds of tissue.
save the bows. meet

the animate organs of my being:

the slow lizard of digestion,
the squirrel on the treadmill
of circulation, the eight-legged
despair that climbs my spine.

say hello, fellows.

'hello.'

the silent one there
is the barbary ape who just fits
the shape of the wrapping.

192800

Cover photograph by Philip Zimmerman

Cover design by Lyn Smith

ITHACA HOUSE
108 North Plain Street
Ithaca, New York, 14850